Copyright © 1995 text and design Milepost 92½

This edition first published 1995 by Milepost Publishing in conjunction with
Arcturus Publishing Limited, and exclusively for Bookmart Limited.
Desford Road, Enderby, Leicester LE9 5AD

Milepost Publishing is a division of Milepost 92½.
Milepost 92½ is Colin Garratt's Audio Visual, Production, Presentation and Photographic Service for the
Railway Industry incorporating The Railway Picture Library.

Designed by Milepost/Wilson Design Associates
Originated, Printed and Bound in the UK by Gresham Print Group, Nottingham

ISBN 1 900193 25 6

Milepost 92½
Newton Harcourt
Leicestershire
LE8 9FH
Tel 0116 2592068

MILEPOST

The Golden Years of
British Steam Trains
LMS

LONDON MIDLAND & SCOTTISH RAILWAY

MILEPOST

INTRODUCTION

The L.M.S. was the largest of the Big Four companies with territory ranging from Bristol to the Highlands of Scotland. Over ten thousand locomotives were inherited in 1923 from some of the largest railway companies in Britain such as the London and North Western, The Midland and the Caledonian. The L.M.S. was a rich potpourri of locomotive design and an extremely innovative railway especially during the tenancy of William Stanier who was Chief Mechanical Engineer from 1932 to 1944.

The Stanier years were one of the most productive periods in British railway history and produced a magnificent range of designs which revolutionised the L.M.S.'s motive power. The 8F 2-8-0 and Black Five 4-6-0s which together totalled over 1,700 engines, rapidly heralded the withdrawal of dozens of outmoded classes. Designs by Stanier and his successors Charles Fairburn and H.G. Ivatt, formed the basis for some of British Railways' standard designs built from 1951 onwards. When the L.M.S. passed into British Railways in 1948, it possesed 7,850 locomotives embracing 100 different designs.

Former LMS compound No. 41162 was a Rugby based engine. She was built by the Vulcan Foundry in 1925 and was one of the last survivors of the Compound 4-4-0 s. She was withdrawn in 1960 and the class became extinct the following year.

Ex-LNWR George V Class 4-4-0 No. 25348 "Coronation" at speed with express passenger headlights. "Coronation" was the 5,000th engine built at Crewe works. She was withdrawn in 1940 after a working life of only 29 years. A preservation attempt was made and the engine languished in store for some years before tragically being broken up. The engine's name was duplicated in 1938 by the first of Stanier's Coronation Pacific's.

Previous spread
Webb built eight 0-4-2ST Crane Engines between 1892 and 1895 for duties at Crewe and Wolverton works. As service locomotives they retained their LNWR numbers in LMS days. No.3249, seen here at Crewe freshly out-shopped, was one of the last two survivors being withdrawn in 1947.

Several London and North Western Railway Claughton 4-6-0s were modified for the Midland Division loading gauge. No. 6005 is seen coupled to a tender from a Great Central design R.O.D. 2-8-0. This engine was replaced in 1932 by a Patriot Class 4-6-0 which eventually became No. 5509. On the left is 1867 built Midland Railway 2-4-0 No. 8, which survived until 1942.

Hughes Crab 2-6-0 No. 42886 and Stanier Class 5, 4-6-0 No. 44747 stand at Manchester Victoria.

This wonderful picture was one of Arthur Mace's favourites. He called it "A Crimson Rambler on it's native heath". Taken at 11am on a sunny July day in 1928, it shows a Midland Compound piloting a Deeley Belpaire 4-4-0 at Derby, the Midland Railway's spiritual home. In the background is a London and North Western Prince of Wales 4-6-0 on a Nottingham to Llandudno express.

Arthur Mace regularly visited Euston Station over a 35 year period and made a series of pictures of trains at the buffer stops. This scene, taken shortly after the grouping, shows a London and North Western Jumbo 2-4-0 acting as pilot to a Prince of Wales Class 4-6-0.

Ex-LNWR 0-6-2T Coal Tank No. 58900 (formally LMS 7699). This well known engine brought a latter day touch of North Western styling to Birmingham New Street where it ended its days as station pilot during the early 1950s working from Monument Lane shed. It was finally withdrawn in 1954.

Opposite
Ex-S&DJR Class 2P 4-4-0, No. 40634 stands at the buffer stops at Bath Green Park having assisted a BR Class 9F 2-10-0 over the Mendip Hills from Evercreech Junction with an express from Bournemouth West to the north.

This is one of Arthur Mace's finest pictures and shows an unidentified rebuilt Claughton 4-6-0 heading a mixed freight. Believed to be a pre-war scene, the engine is possibly the last survivor No. 6004 (formally Princess Louise). The once 130 strong Claughton Class was an epic design in locomotive history and when No. 6004 was withdrawn in 1949 the London & North Western express passenger dynasty passed to extinction.

An ex-London & North Western Precursor 4-4-0 carries out a strange shunting movement in North Wales.

Former London & North Western Prince of Wales Class 4-6-0 No. 25704 "Scotia" heads a stopping passenger train.

Previous spread
Still in Midland Railway livery, Deeley 0-6-4T No. 2004 acts as Derby Station pilot with the works in the background. Known as Flatirons these engines were intended to replace Johnson's 0-4-4Ts on passenger work, but due to a tendency to derail they were confined to freight working. One of the Midland Railway's few unhappy designs, all had disappeared by 1938.

Over page
Ex-LNWR 2-4-2 No. 46757 is seen here in charge of a Stephenson Locomotive Society special which ran over closed branches in the Birmingham area on 3rd June in 1950. Based at Walsall, this 1897 built veteran survived until 1953. One hundred and sixty of these engines were built during the 1890s for branch and cross country work on the former London & North Western system; all had gone by 1955.

A pair of Class 3F Jinty 0-6-0Ts stand as shunting pilots at Crewe bringing a latter day Midland flavour to the heart of the former London & North Western empire.

Crewe based Stanier Pacific No. 46251 "City of Nottingham" stands on the arrival side of the old Euston before that station's drastic re-build.

Re-built Patriot Class 4-6-0 No. 45527 "Southport" heads through Crewe en-route to Liverpool with a Cunard special. The last Cunard sailing from Liverpool took place in 1966.

A Jubilee 4-6-0 approaches Bromsgrove Station having descended the famous 1 in 37 Lickey Incline.

Ex-Midland Railway Class 4F 0-6-0 No. 43940 heads a southbound freight at Evesham. The former Great Western station can just be glimpsed on the far right.

Ex-London & North Western 0-8-0 No. 8942 freshly out-shopped from Crewe works after a major overhaul, is "run in" on light duty. Despite the introduction of some 700 Stanier 8Fs, these classic London & North Western heavy haulers remained ubiquitous well into the 1950's.

This incident at Stafford would have appealed to Arthur Mace's sense of humour. It shows LMS Class 3F Jinty 0-6-0T No. 47649 which has got itself into trouble while shunting a ventilated fruit van.

With the banking engine already attached, a Jubilee Class 4 6-0 takes water prior to ascending the Lickey Incline, meanwhile a Great Western Hall Class 4-6-0 waits with a freight train.

Previous page
Royal Scot Class 4-6-0 No. 46168 "The Girl Guide" surmounts the summit of the Lickey Incline at Blackwell with a lightweight three coach stopping passenger train. The Lickey Incline is Britain's steepest main line gradient.

Towards the end of steam, many locomotives lost their smokebox numberplates as with this Fairburn 2-6-4T standing in Bradford Exchange with a train bound for Leeds City.

Jubilee Class 4-6-0 No. 45576 "Bombay" stands at the buffer stops at number 7 platform in St. Pancras with an arrival from Sheffield. To the delight of train spotters, this engine - along with other Jubilee's named after Indian states - formed part of a transfer from the Scottish Region to the Midland Division in exchange for a batch of long serving Midland Jubilee's.

Stanier Class 5, 4-6-0 No. 45431 heads a special train through Beverley Yorks. This engine was one of the last survivors of the once 842 strong Black 5's and lasted almost until the end of steam, finally being withdrawn in 1967.

LMS designed Ivatt 2-6-2T No.41299 takes a breather from working empty stock trains at London's Cannon Street Station. Having taken this picture at 5pm on the 13th July 1954, Arthur Mace "lost" the film. It was found almost 16 years later on the 20th June 1970 and processed immediately with the happy result shown here which says a lot for the keeping qualities of Ilford FPS.

Hughes "Crab" 2-6-0s were seldom seen working passenger trains on the southern reaches of the Midland Main Line. Occasionally however, they would turn up on specials like this one heading southwards through Market Harborough.

The magic that was once Warrington Bank Quay Station; a Patriot 4-6-0 heads an up express; a Stanier Class 8F 2-8-0 awaits the road whilst Ivatt 2-6-2T No. 41211 performs on the Earlestown push and pull train.

Two unidentified Prince of Wales Class 4-6-0s. The leading engine is one of five fitted with Walschaerts valve gear in 1923/4. This picture is taken from one of Arthur Mace's 35mm negatives, a format he partially adopted in the post war years. The definition compares well with the much larger formats and glass plates of his pre-war work.

Over page
The first LMS Stanier Pacific No. 6200 "The Princess Royal" stands at Euston, a brand new engine in 1933. The Camden shed code 1 was changed to 1B in 1935. The original flat sided tender as applied to the first two members of this class looks incongruous and was soon replaced with the later standard variety.

Ex-MR Class 3F Jinty 0-6-0T No. 47249 undergoing a general overhaul in Derby Works in early BR days.

Possibly on the same visit to Derby Works, Arthur Mace found the cylinders of a Midland Compound 4-4-0. The low pressure ones with a diameter of 21 inches are placed at either side whilst the high pressure one of 19 inches diameter is at the centre.

A line-up of preserved engines in the paint shop at Crewe Works. From left to right, LNWR 2-4-0 No. 790 "Hardwicke"; 2-2-2 No. 3020 "Cornwall"; the Furness Railway 0-4-0 "Coppernob"; the replica of Stephenson's "Rocket" and 18 inch gauge 0-4-0T "Pet". Both Crewe and Horwich Works had extensive 18 inch gauge internal systems on which similar engines were employed for moving components and materials around the works site.

Over Page
With steam drifting helpfully for Arthur Mace, Stanier 8F 2-8-0 No. 48295 heads an up-freight through Stafford. The train spotters perched on top of the wall complete this early 1950's scene when steam trains were going to last forever.

Ex-L&YR 4-6-0 No. 10415 in London & North Western livery stands at the buffer stops at Liverpool Exchange. Note the sign directing passengers to race trains for Aintree.

A traditional line-up amid the interior of the Midland Railway roundhouse at Saltley, Birmingham with Class 3F 0-6-0s, 43435, 43674, 43680, 43620 and Class 4F 0-6-0, 43949.

Rendered surplus on the LT&SR lines by Stanier 3 cylinder 2-6-4Ts, this "Intermediate" Tilbury 4-4-2T of Class 2P No. 2104 has found its way to Mansfield for use on Nottingham trains. Other Tilbury 4-4-2s gravitated to Toton, Leicester and Skipton and the four examples from this last mentioned location ended their days rotting at Carlisle Durran Hill.

Arthur Mace remained active photographing steam until its final demise in 1968. During steam's final years he was resident in Birmingham and did many scenes in the area like this study of Black 5 No. 45058 in begrimed condition ekeing out its final days.

Ivatt Mogul 2-6-0, No. 46492 was one of a class of 128 engines built between 1946 and 1952. These useful light, mixed traffic engines then formed the basis for British Railways Standard 78000 Class.

British Railways Standard Britannia Pacific No. 70046 "Anzac" at Sutton Coldfield in 1962 during it's brief sojourn at Aston depot. Shortly after this picture was taken, the engine returned to it's former home depot at Holyhead. "Anzac" was withdrawn in July 1967 and broken up by Campbell's at Airdrie in January 1968.

Ex-North London Railway's 0-6-0T No. 27514. Although several were transferred to the Crompton and High Peak line based on Rowsley, this engine remained on its native territory at Devons Road Bow.

Another service locomotive to retain its London & North Western number, if not its number plate, was 0-6-0T No. 3323 used as a Crewe Works shunter. This much sought after veteran of the LNWR survived on internal duties at Crewe Works until 1954.

Another Crewe Works shunter of the same period was LNWR Coal Engine, 0-6-0 No. 8245 built in 1889. Not officially regarded as service stock, the engine acquired its BR number 58347. This engine, along with several sisters, survived on internal duties at Crewe long after other members of the class had been withdrawn finally disappearing in 1953.

Crewe Works also employed LNWR special tank number 27334 "Liverpool". This 1867 built engine survived until 1939.

An ex-works repaint at Crewe for Class G2A 0-8-0 number 48899. Built as a Webb Compound in 1904, she was converted to simple expansion 3 years later and was finally re-built with Belpaire boiler in 1941.

The evacuation special of Dulwich College Prep School to Betsycoed from West Dulwich in 1942. The L.N.W.R. Coal Tank seen here would have taken over at Llandudno Jnc. 1995 was the 50th Anniversary of the boys return to Dulwich.

Previous spread
Shrewsbury based Ivatt Class 2, 2-6-2T No. 41203 is the subject of much interest from the local train spotters as it stands at the lengthy platform at Kidderminster with a Severn Valley Line train.

This London and North Western scene at Shrewsbury is another of Arthur Mace's North Wales classics. On the left is an ex-L.N.W.R. Webb 2-4-2T seen with one of that designer's slightly earlier 0-6-2T Coal Tanks.

One of Webb's ubiquitous London and North Western Coal Tank 0-6-2Ts which formed a class of 300 locomotives built between 1881 and 1896. Once prolific across the vast London and North Western territories, most of the last survivors ended their days in Wales working two or three coach branch line trains as depicted here at an unknown location. All survivors had gone by 1958.

An exhibition of locomotives and rolling stock was held at Euston in 1938 to commemorate the centenary of the London and Birmingham Railway. This prestigious line-up is led by Liverpool and Manchester Railway 0-4-2 "Lion" of 1838; Princess Coronation Class 4-6-2 No. 6225 "Duchess of Gloucester" of 1938; George V Class 4-4-0 No. 25348 "Coronation" of 1911 and 2-2-2 "Cornwall" of 1847.

At the British Empire Exhibition at Wembley in 1924, ex-LNWR, 2-2-2 "Columbine" was dwarfed by LMS No. 11114, a 4-6-4T of L&YR design built in that year.

A former L&NWR 4-4-0 heads an express passenger train round the curve into Chester.

Previous spread
Another scene taken from one of Arthur Mace's post war 35mm negatives reveals ex-LNWR Prince of Wales Class 4-6-0 No. 25673 "Lusitania". This engine was one of the last two Prince of Wales to remain in service being withdrawn in 1949. The generic LNWR family likeness with the 0-8-0 in the background is unmistakable.

Over page
Hughes 4-6-0 No. 10452 built by the LMS to L&YR design stands in Crewe Station at the head of an express for Carlisle. After a remarkably short working life, this engine was withdrawn in 1936.

An ex-L&YR 4-4-2 "High Flyer" Atlantic shunting empty stock. Forty of these fast running engines were built between 1899 and 1902, the last one being withdrawn in 1934.

Arthur Mace's station scenes represent some of his most exciting work. Some are topographical, others feature people very prominently as in this one revealing a parade of light engines passing through Rugby led by Nuneaton based Hughes Crab 2-6-0 No. 42888.

LNWR George V Class 4-4-0 No. 25376 "Snipe", a Chester engine, stands on an express passenger train.

The introduction of Stanier's designs during the 1930's led to either the withdrawal of former LNW express passenger designs or their relegation to secondary work as in this instance of Bletchley based 4-6-0 No. 25673 "Lusitania" ekeing out her final days in the post war period with a stopping passenger train.

Previous spread
Ex-L&YR 2-4-2T No. 10872 allocated to Agecroft shed Salford, heads a local passenger train at Manchester Victoria while a near relative in the form of L&YR 0-6-0 No. 52300 stands on a parcels train.